Louis

KÖHLER

THE VERY EASIEST STUDIES

Opus 190

FOR PIANO

K 03589

PREFACE

The following exercises are intended for the commencement of practice in reading from notes, such as is suitable for small children It is taken for granted that the child knows how to hold its hands properly, and that it is able (after having gone through the striking exercises for the several fingers until all five are brought into play) to play up and down with the five fingers one after the other correctly, i e , with a proper lift and a decided down-stroke, with smooth connection and in even succession In doing this, each tone may occupy from one to two seconds Even in case the child does not thoroughly know the first notes that occur, from Middle C to high G on the treble staff, and has only just begun to comprehend what the lines and spaces are, and how the notes are written on or between the lines, and knows, besides, the white keys from Middle C to high G, it may begin to practice the first of these studies If the child has already learned the figures, it will, at first, be guided by them where they stand over the notes; but this does no harm, for in this way the places and names of the notes will be learned, after all, and also the different kinds of notes and their time-value, from the explanations given on new points which come up

Before trying both hands together, each little study must go smoothly and without mistakes with each hand alone; and full time for quiet consideration should be allowed the child for every note, before counting time begins It is of prime importance for the child's progress that all harshness and ill-humor should be avoided; patience and kindness ought to be the invariable rule as long as it is possible to assume that the child is willing to learn In the case of small children practice and instruction should not last longer than a quarter or half an hour at a time, and must cease before they begin to grow tired

Besides these studies, as many exercises as possible should be practiced without notes, care being taken that the scales and finger-exercises are always played smoothly and correctly; velocity must not be demanded as yet—correctness in playing is the main point

In addition to these little studies, pieces for four hands should be played with the child, taking up, as its proficiency increases, the first book each of the following works about to the middle:—Diabelli, Op 149, Practice-Pieces on five notes; Köhler, Op 142, 100 Melodious Practice-Pieces; also Op 124; and, somewhat later, Reinecke, Op 54, Piano Pieces for 4 hands

L KÖHLER.

Studies in the Treble-clef
Stücke im Violinschlüssel
LOUIS KÖHLER Op 190
1.
2.
3.
4.
5.

16.
17
Fine.
D.C al Fine
18.

19. Studies in the Treble and Bass-clefs
Stücke im Violin-und Bassschlüssel

3589

24.
25

26.
27

28.
29.

30.
Fine
D. C. al Fine.
31.

32.
33.
Fine.

D.C al Fine.
34.

35.

36.